The Women's Guide to Getting Organized for Divorce

CHRISTOPHER R. BRUCE

THE WOMEN'S GUIDE TO GETTING ORGANIZED FOR
DIVORCE
Copyright © 2017 by Christopher R. Bruce
All rights reserved.

Printed in the United States of America
First Printing, 2017

ISBN: 978-0-9975316-5-7

Christopher R. Bruce
1601 Forum Place
Suite 1101
West Palm Beach, Florida 33401
www.BrucePA.com

ACKNOWLEDGEMENTS

Thank you to my parents, Russell and Krisanne, and my wife, Ashley. Your continued love, guidance, and encouragement makes me the world's luckiest husband and son and has put me in the position of accomplishing anything I set my mind to achieving.

Thank you also to everyone who has assisted me and mentored me in the legal profession and in life. Especially to my former law partner Matthew Nugent, who for reasons I still cannot figure out, initially hired me in the middle of the worst economic downturn in recent history and gave me the opportunity to learn how to be an effective divorce litigator.

LEGAL DISCLAIMER

This book is about divorce planning and strategy and is not a legal treatise or dictionary. There are many lawyers, books and seminars which do an outstanding job explaining the numerous important intricacies of your state or country's divorce laws. My advice is to hire a competent and ethical divorce lawyer to help you understand how the laws of your state or country apply to your specific situation and to help refine the goals and strategies I tell you to implement in this book. The explanations about divorce law and strategy in this book are not a substitute for hiring a competent divorce lawyer, which is what I recommend you do.

TABLE OF CONTENTS

INTRODUCTION

I am a divorce lawyer. You'd probably be surprised to know that, despite my profession, I am not personally a fan of divorce and everything that comes with it. For this reason, I created the website www.StayMarriedFlorida.com to help people avoid divorce (more on that soon). That said, I believe there is a time and a place for divorce. For some people, the only way to live a happy, healthy and productive life is to end their marriage. These are the people I help in my law practice.

Over the years, I've come to realize that my favorite clients to work with are women who have made the decision to divorce a controlling, manipulative, and/or narcissistic husband. In my experience, these women are not considering divorce due to a desire for money or lust; all they really seek is the right to be happy; to "be their own person"; and to avoid the sometimes every-day experience of being devalued despite their efforts to be a caring partner, parent, and person.

I am passionate about representing women looking to move on from controlling, manipulative, and/or narcissistic husbands because I know these clients are going to have a much better life when their divorce is over. I know by getting divorced, I'm helping my client get through the first stage of what can be a dramatic and positive life transformation. There is something to be said for feeling like you are making a difference in people's lives. For me, working with women seeking to leave emotionally unhealthy relationships gives me "a purpose" and "a sense of meaning" and allows me to really enjoy owning a law practice that is limited to the "uplifting" subject of handling what are often high conflict divorce and child custody disputes.

I've written several books on divorce and divorce strategy. These books are available for free download at www.DivorceInformationBooks.com. This particular book focuses on what women need to know to get organized as they prepare for a divorce from a narcissistic or otherwise emotionally abusive and manipulative husband.

When you expect a difficult divorce, it is critical to "have your ducks in a row" before you get started. One of the best ways you can do this is by gathering the information your lawyer will need to help you in advance, and also by taking some time to think about what you think you might want (or need) in a financial settlement.

We go over all of this in the pages that follow, and I've done my best to write this material in a way that allows it to be useful to you no matter how experienced (or inexperienced) you are in dealing with technology or financial matters.

This book references several worksheets designed to help you get organized and figure out "what you want" in your divorce. If you downloaded this book from the Bruce Law Firm website, these forms should have been included in the email that had the link to download this book. If you did not receive this book from the website, or need another copy of the forms, they are available for free download by going to www.DivorceInformationBooks.com.

This book exists to help you develop and execute on strategies for having the *Best Divorce* possible and optimizing your ability to live your *Best Life* after the divorce is over. Some of my advice may make you feel like you would be "acting like a different person" or outside of your "comfort zone." If you start to feel this way while reading, I encourage you to think about this: being in your "comfort zone" created part of the situation you are reading this book to fix. You are reading this book to become a "different person." To become different, you have to act different. If you approach ending your marriage in the same way you lived it, you'll be as disappointed in the experience of your divorce as you are with your marriage. Revisit this reality each time you feel like you are being told to act outside of your "comfort zone." Use your divorce as the first opportunity to change for the better and not to continue being miserable or allow others to take advantage of you. Remember, the choice to change to a better life is yours, and yours only.

The bottom line is, everything in this book is designed to help you achieve the two goals that I have for all of my clients. The first goal is to help you obtain a divorce on favorable terms as soon as possible. The second goal is to help you lay a foundation for living your ideal life when your divorce is over. If you read this book, and apply my suggestions to your situation, you will give yourself the best opportunity to attain these goals and have the *Best Divorce* possible.

I wish you the best as you begin this challenging but surmountable process.

Christopher R. Bruce
West Palm Beach, Florida

Our Other Resources Designed to Help You

Before we go any further, I wanted to make a quick mention of resources I've put online to further help you navigate the divorce process. My law firm's website, **www.BrucePA.com**, has complementary books, seminars, and forums on divorce strategy, law, and procedure. Also, there are several books available for free download at www.DivorceInformationBooks.com. These books are free and include How to Divorce Your Controlling, Manipulative, Narcissistic Husband, this Women's Guide for Getting Organized for Divorce, our Florida Divorce Law Guide, our guide on How to Find & Hire Your Divorce Lawyer, and Control Your Difficult Divorce, our comprehensive divorce strategy guide.

Also, because it is our belief that the real best divorce is the divorce that didn't have to happen, the Bruce Law Firm developed and supports www.StayMarriedFlorida.com, a website devoted to helping couples build, have, and keep healthy relationships. The website has articles, podcast interviews, and a growing directory of extremely talented results-driven therapists.

Why You Need to Gather Information & Set Personal & Financial Goals

If you don't know where you are going, how are you going to get there? Your *Best Divorce* strategy is designed with the ultimate purpose of improving your life and obtaining your desired financial situation when your marriage is over. However, if you don't know what it is that "you want" when your marriage is over, you will lack direction, leading to both unhappiness during your divorce, and afterwards. Further, if your lack direction, your divorce will take more time, cost more money, and result in more "burned bridges" in your family, business, and social networks. Sound like fun? I think not. You owe it to yourself, your friends, your family, and your bank accounts to figure out what it is that "you want" before you move any further along the divorce process.

This book primarily covers helping you go through the process of determining "what you want" as it relates to the financial aspects of your divorce. To do this, you must first "get organized." You need to develop an understanding of the income, expenses, assets, and liabilities that are at play in your divorce, and to start mapping out the details of some of the trickier issues that your lawyer might need to address, such as tracing non-marital assets and what may be an intentional dissipation or secretion of assets by your spouse. Of course, any great lawyer can do this for you with the help of a competent forensic accountant. But don't you think it would be a good idea, or at least more cost efficient, if you first had a baseline understanding of these issues so that you can help the professionals you hire have a better idea of where they should focus?

Further, you need to be able to then be able to have a "big picture" understanding of all of the information above to help you plan a realistic personal budget for after the divorce and to develop an initial idea of what you want in a financial settlement. Through the following chapters, I'll teach you how to do this. You will be able to understand the basics of your finances, even if your spouse has always handled the money and you've never done anything like this before.

As a warning, the process of "getting organized" and figuring out "what you want" does not happen instantly. You will need to gather and review information related to your marital finances. This can sometimes be a tedious process, but many of my clients find it empowering. Further, you run the risk of being "lost" during your divorce if you do not understand the basics of your own finances. Moreover, you are going to need to know the basics of your finances after the divorce. You might as well learn them now.

Before you take action though, my advice is to read all of the chapters in this section about "getting organized" and figuring out "what you want." Once you've read all of the chapters in this section, you can go back and get to work. By taking this approach and reading the entire section first, you will be able to see the "big picture" of how taking the action steps I recommend will help you be in the "driver's seat" as you move forward with developing and executing upon your *Best Divorce* strategy.

As you are reading this or taking action on the advice of this section you might be thinking something like "What if my spouse finds out what I'm doing?" Don't worry about this. One of the things I'll help you with right off the bat in the chapters that follow is how to gather the information while staying "under the radar" of your spouse and in a manner that allows you to keep everything secure and private.

You might also find yourself thinking things like "My spouse controls all of the information" or "I will never be able to get all of the information that I need!" If this is you, don't drive yourself crazy if you cannot get your hands on everything I recommend.

That said, in this day in age, getting the information you really need can be easier than you think. Even if there are some things you cannot track down, you will at least be able to better "know what you don't know," which can be half the battle in more complex financial situations.

Finally, I strongly suggest that you utilize the complementary tools at **www.BrucePA.com/DivorceBookForms** to assist you with "getting organized" and figuring out "what you want." If you downloaded the book by email, you should have received an email that also included these forms. If not, you can download them from the link above. The forms are free, prevent you from "recreating the wheel," and "take the math" out of the process.

Define Non-Financial Goals for Your Life After the Divorce

If you are getting divorced for the right reasons, then money is not the only reason you are leaving your marriage. For many people, part, or all of the reason they are really pursuing divorce is to have a better life after their divorce. They want to live the *Best Life* possible, a life they deserve, and they know they'll never have such a life if they stay in their marriage. They might not know what their *Best Life* will be like, but they know they want it, and that to get it they need out of their marriage.

The mistake I often see people make is to assume that they will simply "figure out" what their *Best Life* will be after their divorce is over. They foresee their divorce as being complex, and feel that they'll have enough on their plate just to get the divorce done. These people say *"how on earth can I envision what my life will be after the divorce when I still have to get divorced!"* **I strongly believe this is the wrong approach and possibly the biggest mistake you can make in your divorce**. If you procrastinate on figuring out what "you want" your life to be until after your divorce is over you are setting yourself up for failure. Why in the world would you go into what is possibly the biggest financial negotiation of your life without knowing the details of the life you want when the negotiation is over? If you don't know what "you want" how do you even know whether splitting up your family through divorce is what you should be doing?

If you delay defining your non-financial goals until after the divorce you will lack any real "purpose" and as a result risk a financial settlement that has you fighting an uphill battle to make your life better. Even if your financial settlement is outstanding, if you do not define your post-divorce personal goals now you will risk falling into depression after the divorce is over, which makes you more vulnerable to entering into another unhealthy relationship that down the road has you reading this book again to strategize getting out of yet another marriage.

Do things the right way. Figure out what "you want" out of life now. Do not wait until after your divorce is over. Do it now, before you even thing about any legal or money issues. A great way to do this is to meet with a great therapist to help you dig deep into what is making you unhappy and to define what it is that you really want out of life. If you don't know of a good therapist, then ask around. Your primary care physician will know of several qualified professionals who can help you. You can also use my website **www.StayMarriedFlorida.com** to find a great therapist in South Florida.

Once you have defined your personal/non-financial goals, you can move on to the rest of this section for the details of everything else that is involved with "getting organized" and figuring out what "you want" out of your divorce.

Ensuring Your Privacy Part I: The Basics

There is a time and a place to inform your spouse that you are going to get divorced. However, right now, when you are in the initial informational gathering and evaluation stages of divorce planning period, when you still might not even be sure if you want to get divorced, it is not the time to tell your husband that you are thinking about divorce.

If you are abusing a narcissistic or emotionally abusive/manipulative husband, you will almost always immensely benefit from being organized, prepared, and the first to take affirmative action in the divorce process. "Tipping off" your spouse to a pending divorce at this point, before you have gotten organized and refined your goals and legal strategy by meeting with an attorney, is not what you want to happen.

For this reason, it is important to take a few affirmative steps to secure your privacy as you follow my advice for getting organized and figuring out "what you want." Fortunately, these steps are simple even for those who are not computer experts, and in many cases, rely on free software. This chapter lays out the basics for securing your privacy, and the next chapter goes into deeper detail as to how to gather and store information that you can keep private. All of these things are things you will need to do (or at least would be a fool for not doing) after a divorce. As such, you might as well get going with adopting the privacy/security protocols described in this chapter.

As a side note, you should understand that many spouses will be oblivious to you gathering information as recommended in this book. Some of my clients are hesitant to gather the information I advise them to gather in the pre-divorce stages because they believe their spouse is naturally suspicious and will find out what they are doing. I find this rarely happens when people follow my advice below. The reality is that most people who are contemplating divorce are doing so because their spouse does not pay enough attention to them. If your spouse does not pay attention to you to the point of you wanting a divorce, odds are they will not have any idea that you are getting organized for a divorce.

In any event, the basics of what you need to do to establish your privacy are as follows:

Establish a Secure Email Address:

When it comes to establishing your privacy, the first thing you need to do, if you don't have one already, is establish a secure email address. This means that you need to get an email address that you, and only you, view and control. You want to make sure that this email account is not shared with your spouse, and is not stored on any company or employer servers that subjects your emails to being viewed by other people. This step is necessary because your privacy is paramount when planning for a divorce. Especially as your email account will show a trail of some of your other divorce planning activities. If you and your spouse share an email account, or you use your work email, you risk your spouse or others realizing that you are preparing for divorce.

The simplest way to set up a private email is to create an email account at www.Gmail.com. You can set up the account in less than five minutes. Further, having a "Gmail" account will also allow you to get access to several other helpful (and free) Google tools that will be useful in your divorce planning. Also, Gmail has a great feature called "two step verification" that helps keep your account secure. With this feature, logging in to view your account requires the entry of a second (and always changing) password that is sent to you by a text message from Gmail, and you are notified if someone (like your spouse) tries to get into your account from an unknown device or location.

Change Your Password & Email Address in Account Settings:

This should be obvious, but many people fail to do it. As you are planning for divorce, it is time to make sure that you change the passwords on all of your accounts and devices to a password that your spouse cannot guess. This includes your phone, computer, individual bank accounts, social media accounts, and anything else that you would prefer to keep from your spouse.

As you do this, you need to make sure that your accounts and devices are linked to your secure email address, and not an email account shared with your spouse. This keeps your spouse from getting email updates confirming your change in settings and account passwords. One thing to keep in mind while doing this, is that some financial institutions will send out a letter confirming the change in the email address. You might need to watch your mailbox or tell your spouse you are doing this in advance so as not to invoke suspicion.

Secure Your Devices:

Similar to changing your passwords, you need to ensure that your spouse does not have access to what is stored on your smartphone, computer, or tablet, by virtue of device sharing programs like "iCloud," "OneDrive," or other equivalents. Make sure that each device has a lock screen that automatically requires a password if the device has been inactive for more than a minute. If what you just read sounds like a foreign language to you, then you should go to your local Best Buy electronics store and pay someone on the "Geek Squad" for an hour of their time to help you with this. Otherwise, most people at your local cell phone carrier's store should be able to help you figure this out.

Disable Location Tracking Software:

Believe it or not, may people have a program on their smartphone that allows their location to be tracked. If you have an iPhone, iPad, or another smartphone/tablet, there is usually an option to "Share My Location," which shows who is enabled to view your location. If your location is shared with your spouse, they can see you everywhere you go as long as your phone or device is with you. Given that technology is constantly changing, you would be well served to research this issue or to seek out someone who knows the answers. A simple solution is to go speak to someone on the "Geek Squad," which employs people who can help you with this type of issue. The "Geek Squad" operates out of Best Buy stores, but can also arrange to meet you at your home or office.

Set Up an Online Storage Account for Storing Records:

In the next chapter of this book, I am going to walk you through how to gather pertinent records and other evidence in a manner that allows the information to be stored out of your house and office yet still accessible to you on any computer or device that has internet access. For now, all you need to do is set up an account at www.Dropbox.com, www.Google.com/drive, or a similar service. Make sure to set up the account using your secure email address.

Consider Setting Up an Electronic Notes Program:

As you work towards developing your *Best Divorce* strategy, you are going to want to take notes. Some people are inclined to do this the "old fashioned way" by writing out their thoughts in a journal or notepad. My suggestion is that you ditch the paper immediately and move over to an electronic notes program, such as OneNote, Evernote, or the "notes" program that comes standard on most of the newer smartphones. When you take notes with pen and paper, you are "up a creek" if your notes are lost or discovered by your spouse. With an electronic notes program, your notes will be secure and available to you anywhere that has an internet connection. Further, the basic versions of the best programs, including OneNote and Evernote, are free. They also support "dictation," which allows you to speak your notes and have the computer write them out for you. OneNote combined with Microsoft's "surface pro" tablet is great if you want to handwrite your notes but have them kept electronically. An added benefit with using these programs is access to them can be password protected, which allows your notes to be encrypted.

Taking some of the steps above might seem like overkill, but if you want to ensure the creation of a *Best Divorce* strategy, it is imperative to secure your privacy. Additionally, many of my suggestions above are things you will need to do to secure your privacy after the divorce, so you might as well get this all done now.

Ensuring Your Privacy Part II: Keeping the Information You Gather Secure

In the remainder of this section about "getting organized" and figuring out "what you want," I will be advising you on records and evidence that needs to be gathered, reviewed, and ultimately down the line provided to your divorce lawyer. However, before you gather this information, it is important to learn how to do so in a manner that keeps the information private and secure. Fortunately, this is simple to learn, and the mechanics are laid out below.

Step #1: Take all of the steps laid out in the chapter on Ensuring Your Privacy Part I: The Basics.

It is harder to keep your divorce planning hidden from your spouse if you do not get a private and secure email address, change your passwords, and make sure the secure email address is listed as the contact information on all of your new accounts. Also, you need to set up an online storage account. I suggest www.Dropbox.com, www.Google.com/drive (or any equivalent) and there is no need to use anything beyond the free product.

Finally, you should strongly consider setting up a way to take your notes electronically.

Step #2: *Learn How to Use Your Online Storage & Notetaking Programs*:

In my view it is imperative to learn how to use your online storage program (www.Dropbox.com, www.Google.com/drive, etc.). These programs allow you to (1) directly upload and save documents like bank statements, pictures, or any other computer file; (2) to secure the documents; (3) to access the documents from any computer or smartphone that has an internet connection; and (4) to easily transfer the documents to the lawyer you hire to handle your divorce in a manner that keeps them from charging you to copy your own documents. All of the major online storage programs have become popular with millions of people because they are easy to use for people who do not know much about computers. Further, the programs have robust online "help" sections.

Also, I strongly urge you to learn how to use an electronic notetaking program. Preferably you use OneNote, Evernote, or at least the note taking program that comes standard with your smartphone or tablet. I'd prefer you use OneNote or Evernote as notes you take on those programs are stored on secure servers, can be encrypted, and are accessible from any computer. Both of these programs have free versions that are more than sufficient for how you will need to use them. Make sure to enable password protection for your note files to ensure privacy and encryption.

I'd encourage you to try to take an organized approach to setting up your online storage and notetaking programs. These programs are essentially electronic file cabinets for your divorce. So, preferably, you'd want to keep them organized in a manner that allows you to find key information when you need to do so. And on this subject, another advantage of electronic notes is they have built in keyword search functions, which allows you to find information quickly.

Computers have been the "way of the future" for about twenty years now. You might as well adapt now if you have not yet. The small investment of time to learn these programs if you don't know how to already, is well worth not having your *Best Divorce* strategy botched by your spouse figuring out that you are possibly plotting a divorce at an inopportune time. If you cannot figure out how to use these programs, then pay someone to teach you. Call the "Geek Squad" or one of the many other companies that give in-home or in-office computer training for a lot less than you'll pay for one hour of any lawyer's time. In an hour, you'll learn most everything you need to know about these programs and securing your privacy.

Step #3: Gather & Save:

I detail the information you need to round up in a later chapter titled *What to Gather & How to Get It*. As far as obtaining and storing the information, I suggest you use the following approach to give you the best chance of saving information in a secure manner without making it obvious to anyone that you are gathering information for your divorce:

The "direct save" approach: First, try to get the information you need to gather (such as financial documents) in the form of a computer file so that you can save it to your online storage program. Many of the bank statements I'll be asking you to gather can be downloaded right from your bank's website to your online storage account. Further, other documents can be emailed to you and then saved from your secure email account to your online storage account.

The "scan & save" approach: For documents that cannot be provided electronically and are available only in paper form, you should scan the documents into a computer file and then save the file of the scanned documents to your online storage program. If you do not have a scanner, any office services store like Staples or FedEx/Kinkos can scan large quantities of documents into a computer file and then email the file to you. Then, you can save the file to your online storage program. I note that you can use a free service such as www.SendtoDropbox.com to have documents emailed directly from a scanner or email to your secure Dropbox account.

The "snap/video & save" approach: Sometimes, there are documents or files that cannot be scanned. These might be delicate documents, or documents that you do not have the ability to remove from their original location to take to a scanner (these might involve documents in your spouse's private office, as an example). Capturing and storing these documents or files is not all that difficult. Just use your smartphone to take pictures or videos of the documents. Then, save the pictures or videos from your phone directly to your online storage program, OneNote, or Evernote. This is easy, because once the online storage program or notetaking program is installed on your phone, there will be an option to do this by tapping the picture or video on your phone. If you are worried your spouse will access your phone, you can delete the picture or video from your phone after it is saved to the online storage program.

At this point, I think you should know enough about how to ensure your privacy as you go through the process of "getting organized" and figuring out what "you want." Now, it is time to get to work "getting organized," so that you can set the goals for the life you will live after the divorce.

What to Gather & How to Get It

In order for you to develop realistic goals for the financial issues in your divorce it is first necessary to determine "what you have, owe, earn, and spend." In other words, you need to develop a basic understanding of the assets and debts that exist, as well as the incomes and expenses of both you and your spouse. I say a "basic understanding," because, at this point, all you need to be doing is getting educated about these issues. You don't have to be a forensic accountant or math whiz to "get organized and figure out what you want."

Before long, you'll be working with a lawyer and possibly an accountant to help you deal with any extremely detailed analysis required as part of your divorce settlement. In most cases though, there will not be anything incredibly complicated that has to be done, and you'll be able to understand, before you get to an attorney, most of what will be important.

After you work on securing your privacy, as covered in the last two chapters, the next step to "getting organized and figuring out what you want" is to gather the information that needs to be reviewed (don't worry, I'll tell you how to review the information in the upcoming chapters). This information will be analyzed first by you, and will also later be helpful to your lawyer. I note that the information I suggest that you gather might seem to be "a lot," in many divorce cases, you and your spouse will be asked to provide the information I am telling you to gather. This can all take a while, so you might as well start now.

Also, gathering information at this point will allow you to get most of what you need before your spouse does anything to hide information, or cut off access to accounts. My suggestion is to read the rest of this book before you actually gather the information. This way, you will know what you will be doing with everything I'll be suggesting that you gather.

As far as where to go to get the information, the first step in the process should be to see which of the items below can be found in the office or home office, file cabinet, or shared computer. Otherwise, most everything I suggest you gather below, can be obtained directly from the financial institutions or from professionals who would have easy access to the information.

Unfortunately, at this point, you might not be able to get every single item that you need to have a full understanding of the marital finances, as some bank accounts might only be in your spouse's name, or under the control of people who, when asked for the information, might report back to your spouse. This is okay. Just gather what you can at this point, and make note of the documents that you believe exist but are not able to obtain. Down the road, your lawyer will be able to send document requests or subpoenas for any other documents needed to understand what represents a sensible financial settlement.

I encourage you to gather and store the information as explained in the chapter titled *Ensuring Your Privacy Part II: Keeping The Information You Gather Secure.* Also, to keep everything organized, you should separate what you gather based on the categories outlined below.

I am suggesting that you collect at least three years of most categories of records, because that is the timeframe most lawyers are programmed to initially request (you might as well get the information now instead of holding up the divorce later by having to gather documents). If there have not been any major financial transactions, purchases/sales of assets, or suspicions of your spouse wasting/secreting assets, you can consider gathering bank statements over a shorter time period but you should still seek at least three years worth of the tax documents.

In any event, below are the financial records you should gather:

1. *Tax Returns & Related Documents*: Try to get three years of all federal and state tax returns as well as W-2, 1099, and K-1 forms.

2. *Checking, Savings, Investment & Credit Card Account Statements*: Try to obtain three years of statements for each checking, savings, investment, and credit card account. If possible, try to get copies of cancelled checks with each checking account statement.

3. *Business Records*: If you or your spouse owned or recently sold a business then at a minimum, you need three years of tax returns, including K-1 forms, and three years of all records for all financial accounts associated with the business. It is especially important to try and obtain cancelled checks with the bank statements, as the cancelled checks will allow you and your team to determine whether corporate funds were being used for personal purposes. If you have access, you should obtain at least three years of

records from the company's QuickBooks or financial accounting software program. Obtaining a copy of the Quickbooks file will substantially reduce the amount of paperwork you need to obtain. If you cannot get this, try to get three years of general ledgers, balance sheets, profit and loss statements, and financial statements for the business. Finally, it is also helpful at this stage to get copies of all available corporate records, including shareholder agreements, buy/sell agreements, articles of organization/incorporation, and major corporate resolutions, and major leases or and contracts. I understand that gathering these business records can seem intimidating, and that the records are voluminous. For now, just try to do the best you can. Understand that most of this information can usually be obtained during the divorce from your spouse, the corporate accountant, or a lender to the business, who required most of these documents before extending the company a line of credit.

4. *Other Investment Documents*: If you or your spouse are working with a financial advisor, you may have received a personal financial plan or other summary of you or your spouse's income and assets. If something like this was done

in the last several years, try to obtain a copy, if you can do so without making your spouse suspicious.

5. *Wills & Trusts*: Your lawyer will want to see the most current version of any wills/trusts which you created, or which you or your spouse may have a current or future beneficiary interest.

6. *Financial Statements & Loan Applications*: You should try to gather any financial statements and other documents given to lenders, for purposes of justifying a loan or line of credit within the last five years. These types of documents are especially critical, in cases where you need financial support and you expect your spouse to claim their income is less than it really is.

7. *For Safety Deposit Boxes*: Try to find out where all safety deposit boxes are held. If you can get access to the boxes, take pictures of everything that is in them.

8. *Employment Contracts*: If you or your spouse has entered into any type of employment contract or consulting agreement over the last five years, you need to obtain a copy if it is available to you.

9. *Real Estate*: For all real estate currently owned or sold within the last three years, you should obtain a copy of the

closing documents, the deed, any mortgages and promissory notes, records indicating the current balance owed on the mortgages, and records of major improvements and repairs made to the property. If the property is being rented/leased out, you should get copies of the leases, and of any records related to net rental income. Odds are, if the property is being rented/leased, there has been a company set up to own and lease the property. If this is the case, try to obtain everything mentioned above in the business records category for the rental real estate company.

10. _**Automobiles, Jewelry, Collectables & Notable Personal Property**_: For anything you or your spouse own that you suspect has value that needs to be considered in your divorce, you should obtain copies of the records of the purchase price, and any existing appraisals of the items. If there is an outstanding loan related to the property/items (such as an auto loan) get the most recent statement showing what is owed. Also, if the property/items were ever insured, you will need to review the insurance policies to see if you or your spouse ever gave an estimate for the value of the items.

11. *Lawsuits & Judgments*: If you or your spouse have been a party to any lawsuits in the last ten years you should gather any records related to final judgments, dismissals, or settlement agreements.

12. *Insurance Records*: You need to get copies of all health, life, and disability insurance policies that insure you, your spouse, and any children. Make sure to understand whether any of the policies have a cash value.

13. *Promissory Notes*: You need to gather records of any money owed to you and your spouse.

14. *Phone records*: If available, you should get three years of phone records for you and your spouse. These records may not seem important now, but can be helpful in explaining suspicious financial transactions, evidencing affairs, and supporting other issues that might come up in your divorce.

Consider a Strategic Meeting with a Financial Planner or Insurance Agent

Possibly the easiest way to find out the details of the marital finances is to get your spouse to agree to go with you to see a financial planner or insurance agent without any mention that you are contemplating divorce. Some people may find this approach deceptive, but I believe you are not deceiving anyone by exercising your right to learn about or protect your finances. Further, meeting with a financial planner or insurance agent might help you and your spouse get on the "same page" about money issues and joint goals. This can be a great way to possibly save the marriage and avoid the divorce altogether (wouldn't that be something!).

Meeting with a financial planner will benefit both you and your spouse regardless of whether you stay married or ultimately get divorced. Further, if you lack experience handling your finances, you should consider eventually working with an experienced financial planner or insurance agent anyway, and you will need to interview these people before selecting one. Thus, you are not wasting the time of the financial planner. If they are helpful, but not hired, you can pay them for their time by making an effort to refer them clients in the future.

When meeting with the financial planner, there will need to be a detailed explanation of the details of your finances. Usually, the first thing that happens is you and your spouse will have to provide the planner with detailed information about each other's income and assets. Most often, something will be put in writing by you and your spouse or the planner, and your lawyer can obtain this documentation from you or the planner later. After the information about your income and assets is gathered, the planner will work to understand your current expenses. Ultimately, the planner will help you understand how much you are saving, and what needs to be done between saving and investing to help you reach retirement and life planning goals. This will all be educational for you, and can be a "gold mine" of information about your finances if you ultimately seek divorce. You can make the meeting more productive for all purposes by finding a planner that has a process requiring financial information to be provided in advance of the meeting. Later, you or your lawyer can likely obtain copies of this information directly from the planner.

I note that any ethical insurance agent will in effect work as a financial planner, because they need to have a solid understanding of your family's sources of income, assets, and goals to find out whether insurance is appropriate. For this reason, many insurance agents also work as financial planners and do not just sell insurance. The point is, depending on your circumstances, and your spouse's mindset, it might be easier (or make more sense) to convince them to speak to a professional that is known as being an insurance agent and not a financial planner.

A great national company for both purposes is Northwestern Mutual. During college I completed a training program with that company and I was convinced that the company was taking an honest approach to helping clients with their insurance and financial planning needs enough to now trust the company to handle my affairs. That said, there are numerous excellent companies and independent groups of insurance agents and financial planners.

Organize Assets & Liabilities

Now, it is the time to go through the documents that you have gathered to begin determining the assets and liabilities that will need to be dealt with in your divorce. Later, I'll help you do a few things with this information for purposes of helping you come up with your initial financial settlement goals.

As an advance warning, this process can be tedious. However, I recommend that you take it on yourself initially to allow you to develop a working knowledge of your finances. This is the case even if you are not familiar with finances or bookkeeping because your spouse handled everything during the marriage. If this is you, keep in mind that after your divorce you are going to be responsible for running your finances. You might as well start getting familiar with them now. This is not rocket science.

The easiest way to stay organized when identifying the assets and liabilities that will be involved with your divorce is to use a worksheet/spreadsheet to record the different assets and liabilities you find in the information that you gather. I've tried to make this easy for you by including a Net Worth Organizer in an email you probably received when if you downloaded this book. Otherwise, you can get the form at **www.BrucePA.com/DivorceBookForms** (there is no cost for the download). The advantage of using the Net Worth Organizer spreadsheet program is it takes care of all of the math. The program was designed to automatically add up the values of assets and liabilities, which comes in handy when it is time to determine whether your proposed financial settlement leaves you with at least half of the marital net worth. Also, if you use the electronic version of the program your information can be stored electronically and password protected so that it cannot be accessed by your spouse. You can password protect the Net Worth Organizer spreadsheet by clicking the "protect workbook" option from the "info menu" that is located on the "file" tab of the Microsoft Excel document.

The instructions below are based on you using the complementary Net Worth Organizer to "get organized." However, whether you are using the Net Worth Organizer or your own method, the instructions below can be followed to begin identifying the assets and liabilities that are involved with your divorce.

1. *Record the most recent value for all checking, savings, credit, and investment accounts*: In the appropriate section

of the Net Worth Organizer, you need to list each checking, savings, credit card, or investment account. To assist you with the account analysis that will be done later, include the last four digits of the account number in the account listing. Also, for each account listed, you need to put down the most recent balance you can find for the account, and then the date of the account statement used to obtain the balance. If you know or believe other accounts exist, but you have not been able to obtain the statements, then make a listing for the account in the appropriate section of the Net Worth Organizer. You or your lawyer can follow up later to make the appropriate inquiry.

2. *Record the estimated value of all business interests*: List all business interests in the appropriate section of the Net Worth Organizer. This should be done for all interests in corporations, partnerships, or similar interests that are held outside of an investment/brokerage account. It may be difficult for you to value the business interest unless you are the business owner or have particular knowledge of the business' industry. Oftentimes, a forensic accountant will be hired to value any businesses that appear to be worth valuing. For now though, you should try to put down an

amount that reflects the value of the business' assets minus liabilities, which can be found on the company balance sheet or tax return. If you are not able to do this, you should put down whatever you estimate to be the value of the business for now. Make sure to detail how you came up with the value for the business in the notes section of the Net Worth Organizer.

3. *Record the estimated or appraised value of all real estate*: List all real estate (whether a house, commercial or rental property, or vacant lot) in the appropriate section of the Net Worth Organizer. As far as determining the value of the real estate, if an appraisal was recently completed, you should list the appraised value. If you do not know the value, you can use websites such as Zillow.com or Realtor.com to come up with an estimated value. Make sure you write down how you determined the value in the notes section of the Net Worth Organizer. Also, include in the notes anything you think is relevant about the property. As an example, if the property has characteristics that might not be reflected in the appraised or online value estimates (such as extensive upgrades or the need for a new roof) you should indicate this in the notes section of the Net Worth Organizer.

4. _Record the estimated or appraised value of automobiles, jewelry, furnishings, collectables and other notable personal property items_: You should fill in the designated sections of the Net Worth Organizer with the estimated or appraised values of all of your other property and assets, including: automobiles; boats/other vehicles; furniture and furnishings in the home and elsewhere; collectables; jewelry; and any other major assets that are held outside of banks. When you go through this process you should give an explanation for how you came up with the value for each item in the notes section for the item in the Net Worth Organizer. When possible, try to use an appraised value, or get a value estimate from a value estimating service like KellyBlueBook.com. Also, indicate in the notes section any items that you believe need to be appraised by a professional appraiser.

5. _Record Life Insurance Policies_: Record all life insurance policies in the designated section of the Net Worth Organizer. However, only list a value for policies that have a cash value. In the notes section, you should detail as many details as you know about the policy, including the amount

of insurance benefit, the named insured, whether the policy is whole life or term, and when the policy expires.

6. *Record all mortgages or debts owed on real estate and other property*: Fill in your Net Worth Organizer with all of the debts owed on real estate and any other property. Try your best to identify the real estate or item of property associated with the debt. If you do not know the exact amount of a mortgage or loan, but you know one exists, then just write down the estimated amount of the loan and give a description of what you know in the notes section in the Net Worth Organizer.

Once you have taken the steps above, you will have created a concise snapshot of the assets and liabilities that will be subject to your divorce.

Review Bank Statements for Transfers, Withdrawals, & Suspicious Charges

At this point, you should have reviewed your financial records (and possibly some of your spouse's records) to the point of being able to get an initial "ballpark" idea of the assets and liabilities that will need to be dealt with in your financial settlement. This will go a long way towards helping you and your attorney understand what needs to happen in your divorce. Further, by doing this legwork now, as opposed to after you file for divorce, you will likely be positioned to begin settlement negotiations quicker and spend less on lawyer's fees.

The next part of "getting organized" takes what you have done one step further, through a focused analysis of some of the records you have gathered. What I am suggesting you do below does not require an accounting degree. It can be done by anyone. Going through the steps below will allow you to have more familiarity with the marital finances. Further, you will be able to potentially discover evidence of additional assets or expenditures by your spouse, which could entitle you to receive a greater portion of assets in your financial settlement, and/or serve as leverage that supports your *Best Divorce* strategy.

Additionally, if you are still on the fence about getting divorced, the analysis I'll be having you do may lead you to clues as to whether or not your spouse was being forthcoming and faithful to you during the marriage.

My suggested next step is to engage in a detailed review of all of your bank and credit card and installment account statements, including statements for checking accounts, savings accounts, investment accounts, and loans. Your review will focus on outgoing transfers/withdrawals, incoming transfers/deposits, suspicious checks and charges, and sources of payments of on credit, installment and loan accounts. Don't worry; I tell you exactly how to do this below. To engage in the review more quickly, you should read the rest of this chapter before you begin, as you can search for several categories of information at the same time. Also, as you complete this review, I recommend that you utilize the complementary Questionable Transactions Log spreadsheet available at:

www.BrucePA.com/DivorceBookForms

Note: if you downloaded the book, you should have receive an email containing this form.

Using this complementary tool will allow you and your attorney to quickly sort and organize any of your important findings on an account by account or issue by issue basis.

One more thing: if bank statements are like a foreign language to you, put this book down and go to your local bank branch and ask them to teach you how to read your bank statements. Bankers want your continued business, and most of them will gladly take a half hour out of their day to help you understand how to look for what I suggest in the account analysis detailed in this chapter.

Now, it is time to get to work. Here is what you need to do:

Step #1: Review for Outgoing Transfers & Withdrawals:

Go through all of your checking, savings, and investment account statements to review outgoing transfers. For each transfer that is not obvious (such as to pay known bill) you need to see if you see the outgoing transfer is deposited into one of your other bank accounts (the deposit should show up within several days of the outgoing transfer). If you are unable to trace the outgoing transfer as a deposit to another account for which you have statements, then the outgoing transfer may be a sign of a deposit being made to another marital bank account that you have not yet discovered, or of your spouse improperly "giving away" marital dollars. Either way, you need to note all known details of the transfer in your Questionable Transactions Log. As you are going through your statements looking for outgoing transfers you should also look for withdrawals (these would take the form of cash withdrawals or cashier's checks). If you see significant withdrawals that do not appear to be deposited elsewhere, you may be seeing an indicator that your spouse is holding cash or another previously unknown account exists. Make sure to note the significant cash withdrawals in your Questionable Transactions Log so that you and your lawyer can seek explanation later.

Step #2: Review for Incoming Transfers & Deposits:

When reviewing your checking, savings, and investment account statements, you also need to look for incoming transfers and deposits. If the source of a transfer or deposit is not obvious (such as from an employer or another marital account), you should note the deposit in the Questionable Transactions Log. Unexplained deposits could be evidence of either an additional marital bank account or of a source of income to your spouse.

Noting these incoming transfers and deposits now allows you and your lawyer the ability to follow up and seek an explanation later.

As you are going through this process you should know that it is possible to get copies of deposit slips and of checks deposited from your financial institution. If you see a deposit and do not know where it is from, you should try and get copies of the deposit slips and checks that made up the deposit as doing so can clarify what might otherwise be a questionable transaction.

Step #3: Review for Suspicious Charges & Checks:

You need to review all of your bank and credit card account statements for charges and checks that appear to evidence marital dollars being spent or directed towards non-marital purposes. If you see a charge or check that appears to have been for a non-marital purpose you should record the transaction in your Questionable Transactions Log. As an example, if your spouse charged $10,000 at a jewelry store for jewelry you have never seen or wrote their cousin a check for $10,000 for a loan you never discussed, you would want to make note of the transaction. The charges may evidence an affair, or at least a wrongful dissipation of assets that justifies you receiving a credit to compensate you for your share of the money your spouse gave away or used for improper purposes.

Step #4: Review for "Unexplained Payoffs":

The final item you need to include in your review of your financial records is an analysis of the source of payments to all credit card, loan, and installment accounts. What you need to look at is whether you can match all of the payments towards these debts with a transfer/check out of one of the marital bank accounts. Odds are, an additional account exists beyond what you have accounted for thus far, if you are seeing credit card or loan balances being paid off but are not seeing the payments coming out of any of the bank accounts you've gathered. Make sure to note each "unexplained payoff" in your Questionable Transactions Log.

Building Claims for Non-Marital Property

As explained in the Bruce Law Firm's Florida Divorce Law Guide (see www.FloridaDivorceLawGuide.com to download this book for free), certain property is considered "non-marital" and is not split with your spouse in a divorce. Typically, "non-marital" property will include property that you owned prior to the marriage and still own today, property received through an exchange of property that you owned prior to the marriage, and property that you received through an inheritance or gift during the marriage. In most jurisdictions, including in Florida where I practice, you will have the burden to prove that an asset is "non-marital." This means that unless you prove that an asset is "non-marital," it will be considered a "marital" asset and subject to being equally divided with your spouse in the divorce. For this reason, it is important that you gather evidence to build your claims for non-marital property as early as possible.

My suggestion is that you use the complementary Non-Marital Property Organizer spreadsheet available at **www.BrucePA.com/DivorceBookForms** or another organized method to assist you in building your claim that certain property is non-marital in nature. Note: if you downloaded the book, you should have receive an email containing this form.

To assist with building your claim that a property is "non-marital" you need to do the following:

Document property owned before the marriage:

You need to review the assets on the Net Worth Organizer and determine which property you own now was owned before the marriage. For each of these assets, you need to make note of the value as of the date of the marriage, and gather any documents that would prove ownership and pre-marital value. Also, you need to take time to see if you ever added your spouse to the title of the asset during the marriage. Further, if the account was a financial account, you need to make note of whether you ever added property acquired during the marriage to the account. Make sure to record all of this in the Non-Marital Property Organizer.

Document non-marital property received during the marriage:

You also need to review the assets on your Net Worth Organizer to determine if anything was received during the marriage as an inheritance or gift. If so, take the time to gather the information needed to prove that the asset was inherited or gifted to you. Usually, you would have received documents from a probate lawyer, including will or trust documents, that would show an asset was inherited. You may have received similar documents to evidence a gift. As with assets owner prior to the marriage, if the inherited or gifted asset was a financial account, you should try to analyze whether the asset was mixed with other "marital assets." Either way, gather everything you can that helps you prove that an asset was inherited or gifted to you during the marriage, and record the information that you gather on the Non-Marital Property Organizer.

Document non-marital property spent on marital purposes:

While you are working to build your case that an asset is "non-marital" you might end up recalling how you or your spouse spent or depleted assets existing prior to the marriage, or assets that were received by inheritance or gift during the marriage. If what might have been non-marital assets were spent or depleted, you should make note of that on the Non-Marital Property Organizer as well. Your initial notes on this might help your lawyer build a claim that you are entitled to more than half of the assets down the road.

Determine Your Initial Desired Property Settlement

Congratulations! Now that you have went gone through the exciting and rewarding process of identifying the assets and liabilities subject to your divorce, and reviewed your records for evidence of questionable transactions and non-marital claims, you are <u>finally</u> at the point where you are ready to engage in a realistic assessment of your desired financial settlement. For many, this is the most important part of their divorce settlement.

Thankfully, determining your desired financial settlement requires much less work than the "get organized" process you've gone through already. All you need to do to determine your initial desired property settlement is to go through the following three steps:

Step #1:

Go back to your Net Worth Organizer and determine the assets and liabilities that you would like to keep after the divorce.

Step #2:

For the assets and liabilities that you believe are "non-marital", copy the value of the asset/liability into the appropriate column for you or your spouse in the "Non-Marital Value" section of your Net Worth Organizer.

Step #3:

For the remaining assets and liabilities that are marital, copy the value of the asset/liability to the column in the "Distribution" section of the spouse that will be keeping the asset/liability under your desired financial settlement.

It is optimal for you to go through the three steps above in the complementary Net Worth Organizer spreadsheet. This is because the spreadsheet automatically "does the math" for the total assets and liabilities that you and your spouse keep under your proposed settlement. To see this, simply look to the "Net Worth" section of the spreadsheet, which is where the total assets and liabilities appear. If you are doing this all by hand, then you will now need to total up the assets and liabilities that you and your spouse are receiving under your desired settlement.

Now that you have made your "desired division" of assets and liabilities, you need to look at the total "marital net worth" of both you and your spouse. When I'm talking about "marital net worth,"

I am referring only to the amount of the "marital assets" minus "marital liabilities" that are going to you and your spouse under your property division proposal. We can ignore "non-marital assets" from this analysis. In any event, if your "marital net worth" is approximately equal to your spouse's "marital net worth" under your desired property division, then your desired settlement just might be something you can realistically achieve through negotiations. However, if the marital net worth of you and your spouse differs by more than ten percent, you are likely going to need to change something on your proposed property division to make the "marital net worth" of each spouse closer to equal.

As you are creating your desired division of the marital estate, remember that what you are creating is, at this point, mostly for purposes of helping you get organized in developing your initial thoughts on what you want financially out of the divorce. What you are creating now might have some "gaps" and might not represent a realistic outcome. Further, you might need to make some changes to your desired property division based on the after divorce budget that you'll be creating. However, by going through this process of getting organized now, you will feel more in control of the divorce process and will also be more capable of having productive conversations with the divorce lawyer that you hire.

At this point, you should make sure to write down all of your questions pertaining to the desired property settlement that you created. You will bring up these questions as you further refine your desired property settlement when you meet with divorce lawyers coming up.

Create a Current Budget

One of most important things for you to do at this point is to work up to determining your "after divorce" budget. By this, I mean determining what your income and expenses need to be after the divorce, to allow you to live the life you want to live. Taking the time to create an after divorce budget, will allow you to determine whether it is realistic or prudent to take on some of the assets and liabilities in your proposed property settlement. Further, your "after divorce" budget will allow you to understand whether or not you will need to seek any ongoing financial support from your spouse.

The first step towards developing your "after divorce" budget is creating a current budget based on the current total marital income and expenses. Having an understanding of the current marital income and expenses is paramount in creating a <u>realistic</u> "after divorce" budget. You need to know how much your current lifestyle "costs" as you plan out your "after divorce" lifestyle. Oftentimes, your current lifestyle "costs" much more than you think.

The last thing you want to do is go through all of the trouble of developing and executing upon a *Best Divorce* strategy to obtain a lifestyle that is not financially sustainable! Additionally, divorce court judges almost always look to the marital budget (also called "standard of living") near the end of the marriage, as a starting point for determining whether one spouse needs financial support/alimony after the divorce. This means that if spousal support/alimony is an issue, the initial "benchmark" for determining the amount of support will include a focus on the marital budget.

Thankfully, preparing your current marital budget is not difficult. My suggestion is to use the complementary Budget Organizer spreadsheet available at:

www.BrucePA.com/DivorceBookForms.

Note: if you downloaded the book, you should have receive an email containing this form.

My Budget Organizer "takes the math" out of the process for you. Also, my Budget Organizer will be easier for your attorney to understand, as it is in a format similar to the "financial affidavit" you will be required to file in most jurisdictions during your divorce.

As you go about creating the current budget, do not delay the process out of wanting to get exact figures for every single line item. Down the road, there will be plenty of opportunity to fine tune your current and "after divorce" budget.

Once you are ready to go, you should approach creating your current budget in the following steps:

Step #1: Approximate Current Income:

You need to determine the approximate income generated by you, your spouse, and all known investments. If you do not know this information off-hand, you can probably get a decent idea from those tax returns you have hopefully gathered, and any other evidence you can find regarding you and your spouse's income, including the statements for your main checking account. Make sure you make a note of any assumptions you rely on in approximating current income, so that you and your lawyer can later review the assumptions.

Step #2: Approximate Current Tax Deductions:

You need to determine the approximate amount of taxes that will be paid based on the approximate income you are using in your current budget. If you want to make this step simple, you can make all taxes equal to thirty percent of income. Preferably though, you should approximate taxes through a conversation with your tax accountant, or at least by using an online tax calculator tool. I note that **www.dinkytown.net** has a great set of tax calculation tools that will allow you to come up with an approximation of the taxes that will need to be paid. Make sure to make a note of any assumptions that you rely on in coming up with the approximation for taxes for later review.

Step #3: Approximate Current Expenses:

You need to go through the Budget Organizer and do your best to approximate the current amount of all of the expenses listed. You can get a good idea of what these expenses represent by reviewing your bank and credit card statements, especially the year end summaries that some credit card companies offer. If you have the time, you can purchase financial software such as Quicken, which can import all of your financial records and show you how much is being spent on different categories of expenses.

Don't hold up this process to get exact figures for each expense, but at the same time, your budget will be more useful if you put some thought into the approximations used. As with the income and tax approximations, you should keep notes of any assumptions you rely on to come up with the amount of each expense. Keeping notes as you go will make it easier for you and your lawyer to scrutinize these expenses down the road.

Step #4: Review Your Budget Surplus/Deficit:

After creating your budget, you should take a moment to review the amount by which the total income exceeds your total taxes and expenses. I note that if you are using my Budget Organizer, the surplus/deficit is automatically calculated at the bottom of the spreadsheet.

Your current monthly surplus/deficit is a good "reality check" of your marital finances. If there is a surplus, it will probably be easier for you and your spouse to dissolve your marriage without much financial disruption. However, if there is a monthly deficit, there is probably going to be more need for you and your spouse to reduce your expenses after the divorce.

Create an "After Divorce" Budget & Determine Potential Support Needs

At this point you should have developed both your initial proposal for dividing the marital assets and liabilities and your current marital budget. Now that you have done this, it is time to develop an approximate "after divorce" budget for both you and your spouse.

Going through this process, for both you and your spouse, allows you to simultaneously do several things. First, you will be etching out the financial details of the better life you plan on having after the divorce. Second, you will be evaluating the extent that you or your spouse might need alimony/spousal support. Finally, you will be laying the framework for developing your *Best Divorce* strategy by understanding what might be your spouse's economic realities after the divorce.

To create your "after divorce" budget you should go through the same steps you went through in the chapter in this book on creating a current budget. Try to be as accurate as possible in approximating your "after divorce" income and expenses. While keeping in mind that you want to be realistic as to what is financially feasible, this is your opportunity to put together the financial plan for your life after the divorce. As you create this budget, if you haven't done so already, you should be taking the time to research how much your realistic (but hopefully still ideal) "after divorce" lifestyle is going to cost on a monthly basis. This "after divorce" budget should take into account both anticipated any changes in your employment and living conditions after the divorce.

After you have created this budget for yourself, you need to do your best to create an after-divorce budget for your spouse. Going through this process forces you to see the divorce from your spouse's point of view. Try your best when creating this budget to take into account what you are proposing your spouse receive in your initial proposed property settlement. In other words, if your dream financial settlement leaves your spouse with being responsible for certain debts, you need to make sure their "after divorce" budget accounts for the debt payments.

When creating your "after divorce" budget, you will also be determining whether you will need to receive financial support/alimony from your spouse, or if you have the ability to pay any spousal support/alimony to your spouse. If your "after divorce" budget shows a monthly deficit, meaning your expenses exceed your income, you may be in the position of needing financial support from your spouse.

Make sure to take note of how much money you think you need in support from your spouse. You will need to discuss whether such an amount is realistic as you interview lawyers. If you think you will require financial support/alimony, you should carefully examine the "after divorce" budget you created, for your spouse to determine if they have any real ability to pay you support after paying their own expenses. Likewise, if your spouse's "after divorce" budget shows a deficit, you need to realize that you might end up being responsible for paying them spousal support if your own budget shows a surplus.

After engaging in this analysis it might be necessary to make adjustments to the "after divorce" budgets of both you and your spouse. Obviously, you would only be wasting your time and setting yourself up for disappointment if you plan on an "after divorce" budget that is in excess of what you and your spouse will be able to afford. If you are having a difficult time with this analysis you should learn more about the basics of alimony. This is explained in the Bruce Law Firm's Florida Divorce Law Guide, which is available for free download at www.FloridaDivorceLawGuide.com.

Keep in mind that people hire lawyers and accountants in their divorce for a reason! The determination of alimony/support can be one of the more complex, fact intensive issues in your divorce. Your lawyer will help you be able to get help to make sure you are receiving or paying a realistic amount of assistance based on your financial circumstances and the laws that govern spousal support where you live.

Finally, now that you have developed your initial "after divorce" budget you need to reassess your initial proposed property settlement. Take the time to think about whether you are going to have sufficient income to pay for the assets and liabilities you want to keep after the divorce. This is especially the case with real estate. Does it really make sense to stay in the marital home after the divorce if doing so will put you in a "cash crunch?" Sometimes, it might make sense to offer certain "expensive to maintain" assets you'd rather not think about being responsible for after the divorce to your spouse as a part of what they might find a more attractive settlement package. In other cases, it might make more sense to insist upon certain assets being sold as part of the divorce to leave you with more cash, or cash flow.

Summarize in Preparation for Your Attorney Interviews

The final and crucial component to "Getting Organized" is to summarize in several pages the details of what you want, what you need to learn, and your marital history. The purpose of creating this summary is three-fold. First, you will be much more organized by having your goals and questions summarized in one document that you can continue to refer to as you go through your divorce. Second, this summary will be extremely useful as an outline to use when interviewing attorneys (more on this the Bruce Law Firm's book on How to Find and Hire Your Divorce Lawyer, which is available for free download at www.AllAboutDivorceLawyers.com). Finally, the summary you create will go a long way towards allowing your lawyer to quickly develop an initial understanding of your divorce goals and an opinion of whether your goals are realistic.

My suggestion is to use the complementary Divorce Organizer available for download at:

www.BrucePA.com/DivorceBookForms

Note: if you downloaded the book, you should have receive an email containing this form.

The Divorce Organizer gives you the framework for concisely framing your goals for the divorce, listing your open questions/concerns, and detailing the basic information that you will need to have at "your fingertips" as you interview attorneys and move through your divorce. Also, by keeping this document stored electronically, you can continue to update it as you move through the divorce process.

Regardless of whether you use my Divorce Organizer or another method of organization, you need to prepare a summary of the following information:

Summarize Why You Want a Divorce:

Take a moment to detail (again) why you want to be divorced from your spouse and how doing so will make your life better. Forgive me, for a moment, for being a proponent of avoiding divorce unless necessary, but I believe you need to think hard about your true motivation for seeking a divorce. If the reasons for your current unhappiness would be the same regardless of whether you are married, you should consider first utilizing couples counseling or individual counseling before seeking divorce. If you need a referral to a therapist in the South Florida area, you can find one through **www.StayMarriedFlorida.com**.

Summarize "What You Want": Go through your proposed property division and "after divorce" budgets again. Do your best to concisely state the following details:

1. What assets and liabilities do you want to keep in your preferred property settlement?
2. What assets and liabilities should your spouse keep in your preferred property settlement?
3. If you believe that you will need spousal support/alimony, detail how much support you believe you need on a monthly basis, and how you believe your spouse can pay this amount.
4. If you believe that your spouse will need spousal support/alimony, detail how much you believe they will need on a monthly basis, and how much you believe you can realistically pay towards this amount.

Summarize Your Outstanding Questions:

Take the time to list all of your outstanding questions about your divorce and the divorce process. In other words, list all of the things that you feel you "need to know" when it comes to what you should be getting in a financial settlement, and the strategy you should implement to resolve your divorce on favorable terms as soon as possible. Make sure to include any questions that you want answered by the attorneys you will soon be interviewing.

Summarize Your Potential "Negotiation Leverage":

Are there any reasons which make you believe that either you or your spouse might have any potential "negotiation leverage" once divorce discussions begin, that should be included in the development of your _Best Divorce_ strategy? Think hard on this, and detail everything you think might give you or your spouse an advantage in the settlement negotiations. Time spent on this will be well worth the effort.

Summarize Your Marital History: The final step in "getting organized" is to lay out any important details about your marital history, which you believe you or your lawyer should know as they help you develop and execute a _Best Divorce_ strategy. Also, you will need to gather some basic statistical and historical information that your legal team will need to know to fill out court documents and help you develop the appropriate *Best Divorce* strategy. The Divorce Organizer that is available for download at **www.BrucePA.com/DivorceBookForms** lists all of the statistical and historical details you need to include in your summary.

<u>Be Proud of Yourself</u>: Congratulations if you are reading this and have taken the time to act on the divorce preparation materials laid out in this book. While a divorce from your narcissistic or abusive husband will not be easy, you taking the time to "get organized" and "figure out what you want" is will give you a much better opportunity for resolving your divorce on fair terms, as soon as possible.

If you have not yet acted on the preparation steps outlined in this book I encourage you to do so. While it is possible to pay my law firm or any other lawyer/forensic accountant to learn about your marital finances, the direction and sense of control that comes from having your divorce priorities in order -before you even approach an attorney- is well worth your time and efforts.

Our Other Books Designed to Help You

Hopefully you have found this book helpful to you in your time of need. In case you were looking to learn more, I wanted to make sure you knew that this is not the Bruce Law Firm's only book.

The Bruce Law Firm has several books available for free download at www.DivorceInformationBooks.com. These books are free and include How to Divorce Your Controlling, Manipulative, Narcissistic Husband, our Florida Divorce Law Guide, our guide on How to Find & Hire Your Divorce Lawyer, and Control Your Difficult Divorce, our comprehensive divorce strategy guide. When you download the books from our website you'll also get the option for us to mail them to you, or make them available for pick up at our office.

Also, because it is our belief that the real best divorce is the divorce that didn't have to happen, the Bruce Law Firm developed and supports www.StayMarriedFlorida.com, a website devoted to helping couples build, have, and keep healthy relationships. The website has articles, podcast interviews, and a growing directory of extremely talented results-driven therapists.

If you found this free book helpful, the best compliment you could give would be to share our books with others who might be in need (just direct them to www.DivorceInformationBooks.com). Also, we love it when people spread the word about the Bruce Law Firm on Avvo.com (google Christopher R. Bruce Avvo and click to leave a review) or our google business page (google Bruce Law Firm West Palm Beach and click the link to leave a google review) .

ABOUT THE AUTHOR

Christopher R. Bruce is a divorce lawyer and appellate lawyer for divorce cases and has been for nearly all of his legal career. His practice is predominately limited to representing his South Florida clients in divorce and family court matters involving business valuation and asset tracing issues, the need to confront a difficult or intimidating person, the prosecution or defense of long term financial support claims, or serious issues involving children.

Chris takes a particular interest in representing women in divorces from narcissistic or emotionally abusive/manipulative husbands. This is because Chris feels these cases are most likely to result in his client having a dramatically improved and transformed-for-the-better life once the divorce is over.

Chris founded the Bruce Law Firm, P.A. in November 2016. Previously, he enjoyed the pleasure of practicing for seven and a half years with divorce lawyers Matthew S. Nugent and Adam M. Zborowski. Their law partnership, Nugent Zborowski & Bruce, was located in North Palm Beach, Florida, and was limited to representing clients in divorce and child custody cases.

Chris is a native of Palm Beach County, Florida, and a graduate of Palm Beach Gardens High School. Outside of the office, and spending time with his family, his passion is saltwater fishing and marine conservation. Chris enjoys participating in South Florida billfish tournaments and promoting marine species and habitat conservation.

Chris frequently publishes articles on current topics in Florida Divorce Law, and serves as a resource to news agencies reporting on Florida divorce issues. His articles have appeared in the *South Florida Daily Business Review, Palm Beach County Bar Bulletin* and several other Florida Bar publications. A proponent of keeping families together, Chris developed **www.StayMarriedFlorida.com**, a resource for helping people build, have, and keep happy and healthy relationships.

Chris developed **www.BrucePA.com** to further help people create the best probability for making their divorce a *"Best Divorce"* that allows them to move on to a life to be proud about when their divorce is over. The website's resources include complementary books, seminars, and forums on divorce strategy, law, and procedure. Also included is the *My Best Divorce Basics Series*, a complementary fourteen lesson educational course developed around the foundational elements of this book.

If you would like to contact Chris in regards to a Florida divorce or family law matter, this book, or anything else, you can call (561) 810-0170 or go to **www.BrucePA.com.**